READING POWER

Andrew Carnegie

and the Steel Industry

Lewis K. Parker

The Rosen Publishing Group's
PowerKids Press™
New York

Published in 2003 by The Rosen Publishing Group, Inc.
29 East 21st Street, New York, NY 10010

First Edition

Book Design: Daniel Hosek

Photo Credits: Cover © National Portrait Gallery, Smithsonian Institute/Art Resource, NY; pp. 4, 5, 9, 12 courtesy Carnegie Library of Pittsburgh, Pennsylvania Department; pp. 6, 15 (top) © North Wind Picture Archives; pp. 7, 13, 17, 19 Library of Congress, Prints and Photographs Division; p. 8 © Corbis; p. 10 Robert N. Dennis Collection, Photography Collection, Miriam and Ira D. Wallach Division of Art, Prints and Photographs, The New York Public Library, Astor, Lenox, and Tilden Foundations; p. 11 (top) © Alfred Eisenstaedt/TimePix; pp. 11 (bottom), 15 (bottom), 21 © Hulton/Archive/Getty Images; p. 17 (inset) General Research Division, The New York Public Library, Astor, Lenox, and Tilden Foundations; p. 18 courtesy G. Blaikie; p. 20 © Mansell/TimePix

Library of Congress Cataloging-in-Publication Data

Parker, Lewis K.
Andrew Carnegie and the steel industry / Lewis K. Parker.
   p. cm. — (American tycoons)
Summary: A brief biography of the Scottish immigrant who made a fortune in the steel industry and used much of it for philanthropic causes.
Includes bibliographical references and index.
ISBN 0-8239-6448-5 (library binding)
1. Carnegie, Andrew, 1835-1919—Juvenile literature. 2. Industrialists—United States—Biography—Juvenile literature. 3. Steel industry and trade—United States—History—Juvenile literature. 4. Philanthropists—United States—Biography—Juvenile literature. [1. Carnegie, Andrew, 1835-1919. 2. Industrialists. 3. Philanthropists.] I. Title.
CT275.C3 P37 2003
338.7'672'092—dc21

2002000092

Contents

The Early Years

Today, steel is used to make many things. Many bridges, skyscrapers, ships, and cars have steel parts. Andrew Carnegie made the steel trade one of America's largest industries. He was known as the Steel King.

Andrew Carnegie was born on November 25, 1835, to William and Margaret Carnegie. The family lived in Dunfermline, Scotland.

The Carnegie home in Dunfermline, Scotland, is now a museum.

Carnegie (right) is pictured here with his younger brother Tom.

The Carnegie family moved to America in 1848. They lived in Pittsburgh, Pennsylvania. They were very poor.

When Carnegie was twelve years old, he got a job in a cotton factory. He earned $1.20 a week. He went to school at night.

When the Carnegies moved to Pittsburgh, the city was growing quickly. Many people were moving there.

Pittsburgh in the 1850s

Young children often worked in cotton factories in the 1800s.

In 1853, Carnegie got a job as a telegrapher with the Pennsylvania Railroad Company. After a few years, he was running part of the company. By 1863, Carnegie was making $2,400 a year. He was also earning over $39,000 a year from investments that he had made.

Carnegie quickly became successful in his work with the Pennsylvania Railroad Company.

"Whatever your wages are, save a little."
—Andrew Carnegie

The Steel Industry

By the 1870s, Carnegie realized that there would be a great need for iron and steel in the years ahead. In 1875, he built his first steel mill near Pittsburgh. Carnegie used a new steel-making method from England in his mill. He also looked for ways to cut the cost of making steel quickly. He became very successful. By 1889, he brought three of his companies together to make the Carnegie Steel Company.

In 1878, steel from Carnegie's company was used to build the Brooklyn Bridge in New York City.

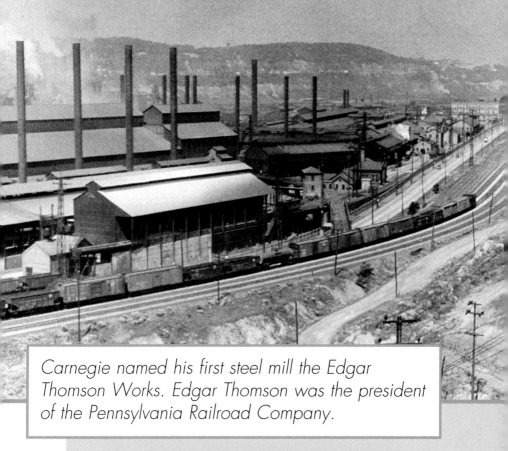

Carnegie named his first steel mill the Edgar Thomson Works. Edgar Thomson was the president of the Pennsylvania Railroad Company.

Carnegie's mills used a new way to make steel quickly.

Carnegie's Family

Carnegie was very close to his mother. She did not want him to get married. Carnegie waited until after his mother died to marry. He married Louise Whitfield when he was fifty-two years old. The Carnegies had one child, Margaret.

Carnegie's mother, Margaret (above), was a very important person in his life. Carnegie named his only child after her.

Andrew and Louise Carnegie were married for 33 years.

13

Troubles with the Union

In 1892, union workers went on strike at one of Carnegie's steel mills, the Homestead Works, in Pennsylvania. The workers wanted better pay. During the strike, there was a lot of fighting. Sixteen people died. After the strike ended, there was no longer a union at the Homestead Works. Carnegie paid workers less and made them work longer hours.

Check It Out

In 1890, the workers in Carnegie's steel factories made about $10 a week. They worked 12 hours a day, 7 days a week, and got only one day off—the Fourth of July. Carnegie kept wages low so he could make more steel for less money. Many people called him a robber baron.

Hundreds of people took part in the strike at the Homestead Works.

In 1886, Carnegie wrote an article in favor of allowing workers to form unions. However, after the strike at the Homestead Works, Carnegie was no longer seen as a friend to workers.

15

Beliefs About Money

Carnegie wrote an article in which he said that rich people have a duty to give their money away to help others. He thought that it was shameful to die rich.

In 1901, Carnegie sold his company to J.P. Morgan for $480 million. At that time, Carnegie was the richest man in the world.

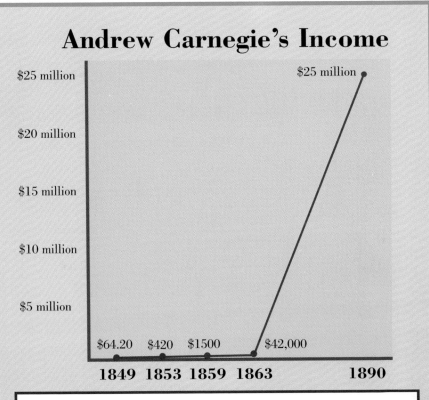

Andrew Carnegie's Income

$25 million

$20 million

$15 million

$10 million

$5 million

$25 million

| $64.20 | $420 | $1500 | | $42,000 | |
| 1849 | 1853 | 1859 | 1863 | | 1890 |

Andrew Carnegie's wages and investments helped to make him one of the richest men to have ever lived.

16

Books and education were very important to Andrew Carnegie.

Carnegie wrote about his beliefs in the Gospel of Wealth.

Carnegie spent the last years of his life giving away his money. His money was used to build more than 2,800 libraries around the world. He also gave money to build museums, schools, and much more. Carnegie gave away more than $350 million in his lifetime.

The first libraries that Carnegie built were in Scotland.

Carnegie gave a lot of money to schools. Here, he sits with Booker T. Washington (left of Carnegie) and teachers at one of the schools to which he gave money.

On August 11, 1919, Carnegie died in Lenox, Massachusetts. Carnegie's work in the steel industry was very important. He also helped to build some of the finest libraries, schools, and museums in the world. Andrew Carnegie changed the lives of millions of people.

> "Anything in life worth having is worth working for!"
>   —Andrew Carnegie

Time Line

November 25, 1835	1848	1875	1887
Andrew Carnegie is born in Scotland	Comes to America	Opens first steel mill	Marries Louise Whitfield

Carnegie spent a lot of his free time in Scotland.

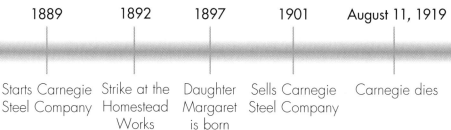

1889	1892	1897	1901	August 11, 1919
Starts Carnegie Steel Company	Strike at the Homestead Works	Daughter Margaret is born	Sells Carnegie Steel Company	Carnegie dies

Glossary

article (**ahr**-tuh-kuhl) a piece of writing

income (**ihn**-kuhm) the money that someone earns

industry (**ihn**-duh-stree) a kind of business that makes a particular product, usually in a factory

investments (ihn-**vehst**-muhnts) things, such as companies, that someone gives or lends money to, in the hopes of getting more money back

museum (myoo-**zee**-uhm) a place where objects are shown and studied

robber baron (**rahb**-uhr **bar**-uhn) a rich person who has made a lot of money by treating others poorly

skyscrapers (**sky**-skray-puhrz) very tall buildings

steel mill (**steel mihl**) a place where steel is made

strike (**stryk**) when people stop working in order to get something, such as better wages

telegrapher (**tehl**-uh-grahf-uhr) someone who sends and reads a telegram, a coded message sent over wires using electricity

union (**yoo**-nyuhn) a group of workers who join together to guard their rights

wages (**way**-juhz) money earned by doing work

Resources

Books

Andrew Carnegie: Builder of Libraries
by Charnan Simon
Children's Press (1998)

*Andrew Carnegie: Steel King
and Friend to Libraries*
by Zachary Kent
Enslow Publishers (1999)

Web Sites

Due to the changing nature of Internet links, PowerKids Press has developed an on-line list of Web sites related to the subjects of this book. This site is updated regularly. Please use this link to access the list:

http://www.powerkidslinks.com/aty/acs/

Index

Word Count: 511

Note to Librarians, Teachers, and Parents
If reading is a challenge, Reading Power is a solution! Reading Power is perfect for readers who want high-interest subject matter at an accessible reading level. These fact-filled, photo-illustrated books are designed for readers who want straightforward vocabulary, engaging topics, and a manageable reading experience. With clear picture/text correspondence, leveled Reading Power books put the reader in charge. Now readers have the power to get the information they want and the skills they need in a user-friendly format.